The Other Man
Was Me

A Voyage to the New World

▼

Rafael Campo

Arte Público Press
Houston, Texas
1994

This volume is made possible through grants from the National Poetry Series, the National Endowment for the Arts (a federal agency), the Lila Wallace-Reader's Digest Fund and the Andrew W. Mellon Foundation.

THE NATIONAL POETRY SERIES

The National Poetry Series was established in 1978 to publish five collections of poetry annually through five participating publishers. The manuscripts are selected by five poets of national reputation. Publication is funded by the Copernicus Society of America, James A. Michener, Edward J. Piszek, the Lannan Foundation, and the Andrew W. Mellon Foundation.

1993 Competition

• *The Other Man Was Me*, by Rafael Campo. Selected by Gloria Vando. Published by Arte Público Press. • *The High Road to Taos*, by Martin Edmunds. Selected by Donald Hall for University of Illinois Press. • *The Landlady in Bangkok and Other Poems*, by Karen Swenson. Selected by Maxine Kumin for Copper Canyon Press. • *The Other Stars*, by Rachel Wetzteon. Selected by John Hollander for Viking Penguin. • *Most Way Home*, by Kevin Young. Selected by Lucille Clifton for William Morrow.

Recovering the past, creating the future

Arte Público Press
University of Houston
Houston, Texas 77204-2090

Cover design by Leonard Broussard
Original painting "The Green Man"
Oil on canvas by Joan Fugazzi

Campo, Rafael.
   The other man was me: a voyage to the New World / by Rafael Campo.
      p. cm.
   ISBN 1-55885-120-8 – ISBN 1-55885-111-9 (pbk.)
   1. Hispanic Americans–Poetry. 2. Hispanic American gays–Poetry. 3. Gay men–United States–Poetry. I. Title.
PS3553.A488308   1994
811'.54–DC20   94-8659
                                                                                    CIP

The paper used in this publication meets the requirements of the American National Standard for Permanence of Paper for Printed Library Materials Z39.48-1984. ♾

The Other Man Was Me

A Voyage to the New World

▼

Acknowledgements

I wish to thank Mary B. Campbell and Eve Sedgwick for their limitless long-distance encouragement and helpful suggestions. I also thank Derek Walcott, Rosanna Warren, Marilyn Hacker and Robert Pinsky for their invaluable criticism, their kindness, and for tolerating most of my medical student's neuroses. My workshop peers—Kathy Coen, Charlotte Gordon, Edie Mueller, Elise Tompkins, and John Whitman—were especially close to the writing of these poems, as were Shanna Byrne, Daniel Bosch, and Jennifer Rose. My family told me all the stories that turned me into a writer.

I am also grateful to the Creative Writing Department of Boston University, for its generous support of this work. *Muchísimas gracias* to my new friends at Arte Público Press.

Finally, I thank the magazines that have published my work.

Some of these poems appeared, sometimes in slightly different forms, in the following publications:

Agni, The American Voice, The Boston Review, Field, JAMA, The James White Review, The Kenyon Review, Negative Capability, The Paris Review, The Partisan Review, Ploughshares, Poets On, Prairie Schooner and *Vital Signs: The UCLA Poet-Physician Anthology.*

This book, like my heart, was made for Jorge.

Contents

LEARNING THE **I.LANGUAGE**

Camino Real

I speak by cutting ruts in air. The dust—
Imagine that it's gold, the Spaniards did—
Is caking in my throat. And when I sing,
Pretend the hawks aren't vanishing, pretend

The fallen fortresses the chaparral
Forgets defend a way of life again.
I speak as if I knew this road. I speak
The Spanish that I never really learned;

The mission walls, spit out like broken teeth
Along the desert roads, are punishments
I can't recall, but vaguely recognize.
The Spanish that I never knew at all,

My heritage and punishment, the walls
At once too sharp and weak to lean upon,
The screeching of the hawks—with these, like them
I want to cut a road, an artery

Directly to the place I know. Pretend
You know it, too, imagine gold is words,
Pure gold is in our chalices and throats,
And watch the mission priests tame hawks for pets.

Rafael Campo

The Lost Plaza Is Everywhere

The protected Venezuela, the rare,
Scarlet birds everywhere—I see it now.
To have a memory is cloudless air
And greenest streets, to have it all right now,
Again, is true abundance! I walk where
Huge mangos sway in every tree, and leaves
Are bigger than my hands, and women swear
At dusty streets clamoring at their feet for laundry
Balanced on their heads, out of reach, in mountains
Crumpled as the Andes. If there are boundaries
To this place, or if really there are fountains
In grand plazas brimming with equator
And the sun the light in every face, I cannot say.
I lived there only as a child. I remember seeing waiters
Dressed in white, bringing demitasse on small black trays,
The wind a vast white hand across the plaza
Touching, for a moment, the café.

Another Poem in English

"The big wave brought you." Borges

Another night, gone. More forgetting of
      the way nights end.

You turned the night to oceans. Wrecked upon
      the bright beach daylight is, I drowned
      remembering.

The birds, afloat like sticks, debris, wash in;
      some garbage is exotic shells.
      The morning, useful, everything
      wanted, clean.

I can't remember drowning, but I know
      my lungs are full of words I want
      to say. "I love you." (How I've failed.)
      I drowned in smashed glass: night and stars.
      I breathe my blood.

The sunrise finds me hemorrhaging, my blood
      is pouring down deserted streets.
      The stray dogs lap me up; the last stars
      outnumber me.

Each night extracts, on passing through us, lives
      immeasurable.

My dream of you is heaviness, stars weighed
        down by the burdensome, dark wish
        I make: I don't want to drown. Night
        outlives us all.

I wonder at the weight of your possessions.
        How heavy is your mirror? Have you saved
        toys from childhood? Please take
        me with you, too

I'll let you wear me, blood-rubies clasped to your lapel.

Illness

Imagine that the bed is not a bed
And illness is a cave, the bags of blood
Stalactites, the doctors eyeless fish—
Imagine that an illness is a cave
From which the body must emerge, but can't
Because the flesh is always so forgetful,
Because a certain greed has brought it there—
A vein of gold, the River Styx, a dream,
Persephone—imagine that the bed
Is not a bed, that God is waiting white
And glorious, and that the beach, which stings,
Is limitless and has no name except
Romance, or sex, just throbbing there all white
Like Marilyn Monroe, Madonna, God
It *hurts*, and then the medication, beds
Everywhere, the cave deepening, the cave
A smile in the Earth: she knows the time
Has come, and she remembers everything.

Rafael Campo

El Curandero (The Healer)

I am bathing. All my greyness—
The hospital, the incurable illnesses,
This headache—is slowly given over
To bath water, deepening it to where

I lose sight of my limbs. The fragrance,
Twenty different herbs at first (dill, spices
From the Caribbean, aloe vera)
Settles, and becomes the single, warm air

Of my sweat, of the warmth deep in my hair—
I recognize it, it's the smell of my pillow
And of my sheets, the closest things to me.
Now one with the bathroom, every oily tile

A different picture of me, every square
One in which I'm given the power of curves,
Distorted, captured in some less shallow
Dimension—now I can pray. I can cry, and he'll

Come. He is my shoulder, maybe, above
The grey water. He is in the steam,
So he can touch my face. Rafael,
He says, I am your saint. So I paint

18

For him the story of the day: the wife
Whose husband beat purples into her skin,
The jaundiced man (who calls me Ralph, still,
Because that's more American), faint

Yellows, his eyes especially—then,
Still crying, the bright red a collision
Brought out of its perfect vessel, this girl,
This life attached to, working, the wrong thing

Of a tricycle. I saw pain—
Primitive, I could see it, through her split
Chest, in her crushed ribs—white-hot. Now,
I can stop. He has listened, he is silent.

When he finally speaks, touching my face,
It sounds herbal, or African, like drums
Or the pure, tiny bells her child's cries
Must have been made of. Then, somehow,

I'm carried to my bed, the pillow, the sheets
Fragrant, infinite, cool, and I recognize
His voice. In the end, just as sleep takes
The world away, I know it is my own.

Rafael Campo

I Don't Want What I Can't Say,
or, Genet on Keats

There are two sides to life. The side where life
Remains unconsummated, reticent—
A shady tree grows there. The other side
Has no beginning, middle, or an end,

It's just the act itself laid bare—a hand
Inside the lion's mouth, extracting what
Our sacrifice demands. I understand
It takes much courage to take out one's heart

And lay it bare beneath the shady tree;
I understand the vagaries of love
And what it means to crave authority.
I still desire what I'll never have:

His perfect body next to me, his cock
And all of its gigantic nothingness,
From what was once a pair, the missing sock,
The memory of shady trees where once

I know I played. But I've heard children scream
Outside within the deepening of night,
And so I realize to intervene's
Impossible—what's lost is lost, what's right

Is necessarily what's wrongly taught.
A parent craves authority and love,
The privacy of one subconscious thought,
And thoughtlessly to give his son the half

Of life he never had. Except he's not,
He's never sure, which one he lacked. The tree
Seems vaguely unfamiliar; the lion's not,
But is ferocious, hungry. Finally,

Not knowing which to choose—as some would say,
Not making clear his preference—the act
Is left unconsummated. Nothing waits.
The shady trees accumulate in tracts

Until they're forests where the lions live.
These lions carry babies in their jaws
Paternally, and teach them about love—
How in our language there are hidden laws.

The Love of Someone

Behind him, saffron hills so passionate
I nearly cry, knowing he was killed.
I read his biography. It is like
Embracing myself—the black hair on our chests
Crackles, mixes, bristles. If I could

Kiss him, I wonder if I'd taste the same
As his mouth would on mine. He would press
Against me, my back against the door,
My shoulders tense as his, my legs
Locked between his legs, pulling at his shirt

As he unbuttons mine. I glance up:
Across the room, I wait in a mirror.
I'm Spanish, the hardcover open on my lap
Makes me pensive. I touch my brown hand
To my face, and imagine that it's always him.

Café Pamplona

I know this really isn't Spain. But still,
You'd think I'd find my father here, his lips
On every cup. You'd think the holly bush
Weren't quite so sharp. I think Rumanian
Is coming from my favorite table in
The back. Are all these people reading Lorca?
My father never orders flan. I have
Café con leche. I'm in Santander,
Before the war. These people reading Lorca
Suspect that he's a Communist. You'd think
The Germans at the table in the back
Would carry out their spying more discreetly.
My father hates the Fascists, but he hates
The Communists much more. The waiter glides.
You'd think I'd find my father somewhere, but
He says he never trusted poets. All
These people reading Lorca would disgust him.
Communists and homosexuals, he'd say.
I order flan. I know this isn't Spain.
The waiter is a hand on every saucer,
Clearing tables, wearing white. You'd think
I'd find him, lips on every wide-lipped cup.
I'm not in Santander. The Civil War
Is over. Lorca's dead. All these people know
The holly bush is sharp. You'd think they'd guess
I'm Spanish, since it's clear I can't forget.

San Fernando

I write to you in English, Father,
Because I am evolving. I'm freer
Than I was before. My hairy chest
Contains a thumping drum, some resolving

Process, a demand to be loved. When you
Fooled me, it was like I'd been to Cuba.
The dark men. The inaccessible island,
Like the parts of you I couldn't see

Beneath your towel. It was cold there,
Or for all I knew they didn't believe in Jesus
Or ate horse meat for supper. You've had us
All confused, Father, for so many years

I can almost imagine centuries. I know
Almost the knife of your exile,
How you lost your middle name in the sea
On a ninety-mile journey. In your smile,

That relic of your happiness, I see
A businessman, my dad, a broken Catholic man
Who had servants once. I save the parts of you
You let me have, like shards of pottery,

Like fragments of my own puzzle. I think
I found them in some abandoned plaza.
The wind that blew behind Columbus
Defined my back. I cried into this ink,

Dipped my pen, and saw you. Father,
You were naked, my martyr, hot coals
Awaited you somewhere. Your mouth opened,
As if to tell me something you'd forgotten.

What I saw was dust rising distantly.
Small frogs chirped in dry trees. I scratched
Over this page, until your eyes stopped me.
I'll keep this with the things I save, for you.

Belonging

I went to Cuba on a raft I made
From scraps of wood, aluminum, some rope.
I knew what I was giving up, but who
Could choose his comfort over truth? Besides,
It felt so sleek and dangerous, like sharks
Or porno magazines or even thirst—
I hadn't packed or anything, and when
I saw the sea gulls teetering the way
They do, I actually felt giddy. Boy,
It took forever on those swells of sea,
Like riding on a brontosaurus back
Through time. And when I finally arrived,
It wasn't even bloody! No beach of skulls
To pick over, nothing but the same damn sun,
Indifferent but oddly angry, the face
My father wore at dinnertime. I stripped
And sat there naked in an effort to
Attract some cannibals, but no one came;
I watched my raft drift slowly back to sea,
And wished I'd thought to bring a book
That told the history of my lost people.

In the Form

A sonnet? Tension. Words withheld. A rhyme
Where memory has left its watermark,
A turn of phrase that brings another time.
(My parents arguing about the stork,
And whether it appears in Shakespeare's work:
"Let me not to the marriage of true minds—"
"That's enough, dear!") A passion gone berserk,
A whetstone where the ax of language grinds
Until precision is its point, until
The carving out of one's own heart is fine
And painless as a summer's breeze. Control
Is what I shout into this microphone
About: I want to say I love them. Wait,
I can't—I'm running out of time! Too late.

II. FAMILIA

SONG FOR MY GRANDFATHER

I. Guantánamo

My oldest country lies before me now.
The barren salted plain—his chest, I saw,
Which hides the crab that rattles with its claw
The rosary it stole from him. In the town
My oldest country will forever mourn,
Where the strongest sun laid two hot palms
Across his chest, where the ocean calmed
His fears of death, I was born when he was born.
When he dies, I must find the rock beneath
The mango tree. Beneath it he has left
His shoes, his razor, and a note he coughed
Through his cigar, in Spanish. I will read
Until the sand has swallowed me—today,
Perhaps, when he tries to grasp my hand
Again. His chest, my dying grasslands.
His rosary rests in a silver tray.

II.   The Medicine Cabinet

When I was weed-tall, I wondered whether
He could see in Spanish. I wandered
In his bathroom, where the tree squandered
Guavas obscenely and the fogged windows
Let me see. Digoxin, the dark bottles
Señor Méndez gave him, the cheap cologne
He seldom used—all his spirits overgrown—
His walker, like a cage of metal,
To help him off the toilet. In Spanish,
If he did see that way, there was no word
For walker. I prayed he never learned
To say it when my Grandma fell. English
Has its way of blinding, even saving,
When you speak it. I wondered, climbing higher
On the toilet, why it saves the liars—
Why I should live while he was dying crazy.

III.   The Cure for Cancer

The pool is clear, like the aqua lozenge
I wish I had to give to him. The cure
For never speaking English well, the sure,
Cool medicine, the steady, menthol revenge
Of white Miami melting on his tongue.
I hated him for that, hated him for what
He made me do. Like the time we ate
Soft Cuban bread beneath the palms–he sang
"Yo soy un hombre sincero." Like the time
The hissing came, and the mechanic
Overcharged. Like the sharp metallic
Taste of the food he cooked–a dash of wine
The bloody gush of tears the black beans
Took–in the well-worn pan they owned. I know.
I forgive myself the seedling that I grow
Inside my heart that gives no shade to him.

Rafael Campo

IV. Grandfather's Will

On the subject of your inheritance:
I give you the plantation. I give you
A seed inside your penis. I love you.
I leave you all the dark significance
Of things like candles, the small metal pin
Inside my hip, the dusty house in Spain.
I leave you the plantation, and the pain
Of sugar. I leave you even the scattered sins
Of island life: thirst in spite of water
Everywhere, to not escape, and to think
You rose above the sea on purpose. Tanks
Are crushing my body now—the traitors
In our house have come for me. A word of caution:
Remember me. Bury me in the ocean.
Burn me to brown sugar—drink me, a potion
In your coffee. It grows on your plantation.

V.   The Cockroach Came

He's dead now: there, I saw the shadow move
Across the wall. The wallpaper, orange
As chemotherapy, or him, deranged.
A gurgle. Bald, his head is strangely smooth.
In the kitchen, they're still preparing dinner
For him. My father grinds the rice and beans
Himself. On his bald head, the sweat I've seen
More often lately. He's gotten thinner.
He looks toward me, like I'm the shovel
He can dig with for the truth. "My son,"
He seems to say, because his father won't,
Or can't. Or won't. Then, I hear the gravel
Grinding in the driveway. Is it more groceries?
His favorite *pastelillos*? But he's dead—
No voice is left to write this poem. The bed.
His bed. And a cockroach on the laundry.

Rafael Campo

VI. Roses in Little Havana

Because the roses were deforming sunlight
Perfectly, because six roses made
The inward thing of which I'm so afraid
From the light where he lay sick, I might
Have cried. As if sickness were that shade of pink,
Or that rim of pink around his eyes a way
To circle then the most important grey
I'll ever know. It was time for me to think
Of things like his garage, water never
Ends, the recession, what will come again.
Having nothing I would still defend,
I made my knee become imperfect lever
To my world: I knelt, the world moved—I see
Him say, his lips chalk trying hard to draw
The words on air, the roses still as awe:
"You must stay, to watch me die in peace."

VII.   His Face

In the distance, it looks like just another fist,
Or the shrunken heads of cannibals
Or the knot inside when I've seen lab animals
Efficiently killed. He has an awkward twist
That was sculpted by the prison guard
Upon his nose. When he bled he must have thought
They were killing my Aunt Mary, or they'd brought
My grandmother to the military base, hard
Between their legs. She was beautiful.
His face still searches hers, for the single line
They left for him to find. His face is time
Walking on skin. His face is like the pitiful,
Drying mud on his plantation, which he would die
To save, even now. Which he dies to save.
Each breath another old attempt in vain
To hold her under lemon trees and cry.

VIII.   His House in Spain

He asked me, stooping over whatever
He's been pushing all these years, if I
Knew where Spain was. So I searched the dry
Places of my mind: the Sahara desert,
Death Valley, the Havana they had carried
Back here to Miami. I was twelve, so my maps
Were small. My mother was beneath a fan,
In the nap she brought from her New Jersey
To protect herself. He'd brought me to the tree
That he said looked like Spain. Some rare bird
Clung to a branch, like it was every care
In the world. The bird cawed. He looked at me.
I don't remember what I said, or I said
"I don't remember, Grandpa." His finger
Poked my chest so hard, so much stronger
Than my bone, it left this mark: "In here," he said.

IX.   Miami Se Habla Español

When I'd see this sign in big store windows—
Grandpa entered only these—I'd imagine
That a secret message was in passion
Being sent to Earth, to our blue Pinto
We'd travelled in from planets killed by growth.
I would sit beneath the steering wheel
In my cockpit, pressing down on where his heel
Made the car slow down. Fearless, free, we'd flown
Through ninety hazy nebulae; our sun
Was much, much hotter, which was why we chose
Miami. Then I checked the dials and I closed
The air-locks tight. The radio—chrome—one
Dial that could end it all. We could
Contact them with it—they would sing to us
If ever we felt too lonely here, or lost
Near death. Our language was our secret code.

X. 10509 SW Terrace

Yellow stucco, swirling hot—it burns to lean upon.
House after low house, all pressed down by sun.
Across the street, Tío dies in his room
With the crucifix above his head. When
Next door, where the steam is reaching out
From an open window, Tía Yoya
Simmers *caldo gallego*, while Goya
Boils darkly in her mind. She's getting out
To art museums, Bingo Latino,
And the mambo dance for seniors Thursdays.
Her bones are so fragile from steroids
I could break her right in two. Like I do
This lizard, sunning green on the stucco
Like a shaving of Cuba, or a dream
The dinosaurs had of surviving. The steam—
For lunch, Grandpa mashes boiled yuca.

XI. Anatomy Lesson

"Examine him," my father said. "That alone
Will make him better." So I looked. My hands
Were ordinary hands—you understand
He was my grandfather. Once he'd been blown
Here from some island, like seeds or twigs
Or an exhausted egret. I looked again.
My chest was just an ordinary blend
Of startled breath, some courage, and the legs
To run off in the opposite direction.
I looked for one last time. What I saw
Was skin falling from bones; the scars I saw
Made me wince. I said, "This reflection
Is not of me," as my hands touched him once
Where the swelling was, once where it hurt him,
Once where he said he couldn't feel—then, certain
And soft as egret's wings, my hands flew off.

XII.   Cuban Poetry

My grandfather loved my grandmother.
My uncle is an alcoholic. My aunt
Looks so much like my father, I can't
Understand why they hardly speak. My mother
Is from New Jersey. She hates the heat.
Her skin is whiter than my other aunt's,
Who was killed by a drunk driver. I can't
Understand why they never hate, why they speak
Spanish like it was butter knives, not plates
Hurled at the children. My cousin married Joy,
Who is blonde. Her friend was raped by a boy
Wearing camouflage, in the parking lot by Ames.
My mother cried for her. She is white, so white
I keep expecting her to melt, or faint.
My father holds his briefcase, like a saint
Who can't save anyone. Grandpa died last night.

XIII.   The Funeral

His corpse: the blood and bitterness have left
This residue. The fiery red carnation,
Like the impending, final conflagration,
Is the only thing I want to take. I dread
Not looking like a man myself. I kneel;
The coffin ascends. I eat the bread of him:
The suffering, the hands that held me pinned
Against his chest where trembling I could feel
His heartbeat tap against my ear, the way
He died so silently I didn't hear.
He looks so much like Franco, then my dear
Federico—I don't know yesterday
Isn't the flower blooming on his black lapel.
How could I know that hell is not the burning
In both my knees. My face is just the turning,
The constant turning from him as he fell.

XIV.   The Things I Don't Remember

His cufflinks. (He wore cufflinks made from shells.)
Exactly where the mole was on his face.
His smell. His smell. That rubber thing in the place
He kept everything useless. The hotel
In the wine-stained postcard taped to his mirror.
(He stayed there with his family once.)
The proper use of the future-perfect tense.
(He taught me that.) How I failed to cure her.
(My grandmother got sick when I was still
In medical school.) Which finger it was
That he lost. And if he lost one. (Because
He had no doctor there?) Why we kill
The things we want to know. Why that stain.
Why I still want to remember the three words
He always said to me in English. The herd
Of goats I dreamt he raised. The rubber thing. Spain.

XV.   The Decline of the Spanish Empire

The willows in the park across the way
Forever searching seconds in green wind.
Signs on highways pointing out New England;
The vegetation seemed to die away.
Clunking cowbells signal unseen movements.
On the board a teacher writes: RAPHAEL,
SALLY, MILDRED, KELLY, BRADLEY. Steel
Rivets hold my desk together. Bent
Against the podium, he has lectured
Like the ancients. He mentions the Third World.
I am missing points, every third word,
Worlds I never knew existed. I venture
That my grandfather came from Santander.
That he swears most elegantly in Spanish.
They regard me. "They were very foolish,"
He begins again, "not to see what they'd conquered."

XVI.   Sonnet for My Grandfather

My oldest country lies before me now.
In the distance, it looks like just another fist
To help him off the toilet. In Spanish,
I forgive myself the seedling that I grow
Exactly where the mole was on his face.
I don't remember what I said, or I said
"I scream so loud, I write this poem." The bed.
My father holds his briefcase, like a saint—
Because the roses were deforming sunlight,
Forever searching seconds in the wind
Of sugar. I leave you even the scattered sins
Next door, where the steam is reaching out,
To run off in the opposite direction,
Near death. Our language was our secret code,
Is the only thing I want to take. I dread
He's already written it on my plantation.

SONG FOR MY FATHER

I. My Father's Childhood

A beach. A cliff like walls, unscalable
Gray walls, behind him everywhere. The beach
Dissolves by days. Each day dissolves in bleach
That's made from salt, the sea, the powerful
Sun's rays. The cliff provides no shade. The salt
Finds ways inside his wounds, deposits pain
The shape sharp crystals are against the grain
In human wood: his nerves, his veins. Basalt,
Black rock he isn't made from, forms the cliff.
His castle grew from sand, small hands, unkind
Thoughts boys will sometimes have, and shells. Downwind,
The secret man. He stands, an obelisk
Made dark and pointed by the sun beyond,
Behind him like a cliff of marble slabs.
He's knife-faced, dark, tradition come to stab
The wind for me, his son, to touch his son.

II. Keats and Shakespeare

They met, their college English class like light
Illuminating their emotions. Dates
Evolved from reading poems, their homework Keats
And Shakespeare, their homework deepening nights
Until they found each other's arms could grasp.
My mother thought his accent made him hers
To teach; my father thought his accent turned
A different shade of red with her, not the blush
Of shame, but the rose of love. They shared their books.
She cooked spaghetti once; another night, her skirt
Was black and looked so innocent it hurt
His eyes. They'd read until his heart unhooked
And rocked and rocked inside his chest, the sounds
Her breathing made so much the shape of hands
To hold her voice, and English understand,
Was what he'd dream he might have never found.

III.   Planning a Family

I wished to make a boy from her, a son
Of numerous abilities, a true
American, the way I could salute
The country that had rescued me. A son
Who wished to please his father, too, I knew
This future son would learn the language well,
And speak respectfully to me, and tell
The truth no matter what they taught in school—
He'd go to Harvard, tall with scholarships;
Become a doctor (blood of course a thing
He'd never shy away from); grow the wings
I never had—I never had like steps
Ascending betterness before my feet.
Because I ached to climb beyond, I ached
To have a son to love what I can't hate,
To teach me my own life, to share my grief.

IV. Family Dinner

With dinner, questions came: geography,
World capitals, New Jersey's county seats,
And all the teams the New York Yankees beat—
World Series *and* the playoffs. History
Was lurking in my mother's gravy boat:
"You know the names Columbus gave his ships?"
Potatoes meant biology, like which
Deficient vitamin could cause the growth
Of hair on tongues, or bones to curve and bow—
The children's malformed legs wide mouths that screamed
In nightmares I would have. Desserts' whipped cream
Was mountains lost explorers climbed, or snow
That drowned each careless British admiral,
Whichever pole he sought. My father taught
His sons that wrongs would be corrected; thoughts
Were mending bones; what meats were which animals.

V. Their Long Vacations in Hawaii

The slide projector always seemed a trap
My father tried to pry us from, upset,
His pen-knife magnified a size so great
To watch the ceiling frightened me. His lap
Was occupied with future carousels;
So I would sit remorsefully between
My brothers, Steve and Mark. Inside the screen
I wished I could dissolve. The frozen world
Of white would change with every sudden click:
The house where he had held me in his arms,
Their long vacations in Hawaii, farms
He said belonged to us before the trick
Of history had happened and we lost
It all. And then another click, and then
We lost it all, again. He'd clean the lens—
Slides, chipped from time's vast glacier gliding past.

VI.   Advice for the New World

I populate with you, my son, this place.
My feet found clefts in the cliff dividing you
From Cuba—then, I raised my eyes straight through
The blazing curtain of the sun, its lace
Of clouds, and saw this continent above.
My island wouldn't budge. Dictatorships
Resembled oceans, sweeping waves of fists,
The poverty was like a ship that plunged
And flew and always opened like a wreck.
My voyage ended here. I lost it all.
My family's wealth, the ruby of my health,
The golden statue of my love, the stacks
Of slides in carousels. My son, advice
Is all that's heavy in my pocket now:
You must learn the art of moving islands, towns
You must transport; make kneel the precipice.

VII. Honest

All honesty is made from fear of shame.
I feared my father was ashamed of me.
My father always seems so honest. He's
My homonym: he gave to me his name.
I guess I'm being honest when I say
I was in love with him when I was young;
I was afraid he'd be ashamed his son,
On whom he'd practiced so much strength, was gay.
I fear my honesty may cause us pain.
My father is a gentle, private man.
I know he loves me. That in him I can
Entrust my very soul. Instead, complain
He never understood until I left
His home is what I've done. My pretty verse,
So fearful, shameful—honest, yet perverse—
I offer him, as though it were a gift.

VIII.   My Father's View of Poetry

You can't make much to live on doing it.
You can't. You can't tell stories—poems fight
A narrative. You surely can't cure night's
Forgetfulness with it, or say with it
Important histories and truths. You can't
Make money writing it. In medicine
You lay your hands on people just the same.
You think you are a poet? No, you don't
Know English well enough. You don't know days
Begin to feel thin, like atmosphere
Ten miles high above the monstrous tear
The earth will always be. And yesterday
Is better off forgotten. When you die—
I've seen a revolution, so I know—
You're never counting syllables. You know
The murderers will drain your throat of sighs.

IX.   My Patient's Heart Attack

His room is just like Mrs. Hanson's room.
The window barely keeps the city out.
I want to feel some pity now, or shout
So loud for justice clouds will be subsumed
In me, my voice like oceans on the rise.
I know that patients die. I see the lines
The pillows leave imprinted, humankind
Around me, in his self-inflicted eyes
The wounds of sixty-seven years. I see
The disappointment on his wedding day,
The deep resentment of his son who's gay—
They look alike—the undeniably
Successful way he made careers unfold
Like blankets spread with silver lamps. The room
Is cold, and now, like every other room
Containing dying life, it seems to grow.

X. On Vacation from Medical School

His EKG is unfamiliar ground.
He shows it to me on the day the end
Of my familiar ground becomes a bend
I cannot follow round. A well-defined
Infarction happened here. I don't know when.
I try to think of times I wished him dead,
Each knife in outline here. The line deflects
Each time his heart's electric waves begin
To rise, from unknown caves in cliffs, my screams
About to swallow him. The unfamiliar ground
Of words he never spoke to me, whose sounds
Are echoes in my ears—his arms through me
My blood, his EKG is mine, his heart
Was touched by me, I swallowed him in dreams
Of Cuban soldiers, hate, and curing heart disease.
His EKG. My love seizes me in bursts.

XI.   What My Mother Says

She gazes at him, pure, an urgent light.
My mother's still in love. I fear for her,
Since so much love's impossible—the years
Like hands in everything pushing them apart,
Her fear she's less attractive now, four kids
With hands on everything inside her bent
On taking sides in fights, and making dents
In the fragile package that their marriage is.
The way she gazes, she could cure the stars.
She can. She tells him anything. That sins
In sons can be forgiven, that Disneyland's
Affordable, that cars are only cars
But people can't survive the dents. She went
To visit, gazing at the stars that night;
The stars were bathing in her tears. Tonight
I think of how she loves him, but I can't.

XII.   Love Poem

My father is another man I love.
I love another man. My father is
A man who loves his parents, wife, and kids.
I am his son. The other man I love
Is someone very much like him, a man
Of honest words. And strong commitment. Love
As deep as his. Except it's mine to have.
My father knows this man. My father can
Make fists from words. He is a man I love;
I help him with his fists. I am his son.
I am his son. My father knows I run
Away in his direction. That I love.
That words I make are only words, that sons
And fathers love enough so that a knife
Can grow between two men, and take one's life.
I love my father. I am not alone.

XIII. I Dream I'm Him

It starts like this: my superstitious aunt
Reminds me that our father killed a goat
When I was born. The strangest type of art
Is hanging on the walls—it's made of taunts
My classmates scream at me. She says, in Greek
That's like some other foreign language, "The goat
Was wrongly sexed. It was a lamb. It fought.
This means your eldest son shall never speak
Your native tongue, and love you like a wife."
She stubs out her cigar; I've grown to be
A gorgeous man. I'm mute. Then, gradually,
Like stars upon the namelessness of night,
I realize I'm him. Except reverse
Is forward here, I'm back to Cuba's poor,
Untillable soil, my hoe in hand—a door
Beneath my feet that vomits lambs in herds.

XIV.   I Imagine He Is Ill

My father worried over colleges
I might attend, the weekend she arrived.
"The applications made a pile so high
I almost missed your sister's day," he says,
From deep inside the hospital bed. She's twelve
Today, and doesn't understand her gift,
That he's alive. Today, my father wished
To see her graduate, and worried while
They pressed the stethoscope to him. Until
Today, when I saw the tubing taped to him,
I didn't understand how much I'm him,
How much I'm parts of him: my will
Across his face; my knowledge knees he prays
Upon for me; my eyes the green his life
In Cuba was; my lungs his songs. Her birth
Reminds me we're his heart, and what it means to break.

XV.   Untitled

They named me after him, and then he changed
His name. I learned my changing names. In school
Kids called me Ralph; in college, they said Rafael.
My naming never bothered me; that hinged
Upon the lesser issue. But what *did*
Was changing his on me, while changing him
To me. (The surgery shall now begin.)
I don't deny the right to change the grid
One plots one's life along. I know it killed
My grandfather, that island like a fang,
The whole impoverished sea a mouth of dung
And broken teeth. Extraordinary skill
Was what enabled him to stitch that wound
And change his name, like sewing on a patch.
Then, to me he held the blade, struck a match,
And sterilized it. I hardly bled or made a sound.

XVI. Sonnet for My Father

The secret man. He stands, an obelisk
When I was born. The strangest type of art
Was black and looked so innocent it hurt.
He never understood until I left
It all. And then another click, and then
The disappointment on his wedding day—
They named me after him, and then he changed
The country that had rescued me. A son
Was mountains lost explorers climbed, or snow.
I try to think of times I wished him dead,
A man who loves his parents, wife, and kids.
You think you are a poet? No, you don't,
Since so much love's impossible—the years
Resembled oceans, sweeping waves of fists.
That he's alive today—my father wished
To give me continents of love—is clear.

SONG FOR MY LOVER

I. The Consequences of Love

The narcissism universally
Attributed to infants once belonged
To me. I was an infant once; the throngs
Of infants in my lungs were savaging
The air with cries. My mother sang. I cried
Amazing revelations, primitive
Love songs, then tried my hand along the edge
Of separation. Dead—I'd been the bread
She baked, I'd been the rose that poured like wine
And thorns between her muscular legs—and now
I dropped until my cradle like a cloud
Suspended me, or broke my fall. The climb
Since then miraculously has an end.
In the mountain of my heart, I sink like spikes
The lover who, I desperately hope, takes
Our love to a height where no descent begins.

II.   What I Learned from My Parents

Besides that anger in the kitchen drawers
Is dangerous, and hopelessness resides
In subdividing closet space: inside
The heart of every lover hide the pearls
The lover wants to give away. They're smooth
From all the agony of wanting love,
From clenching year by year, dove by dove,
One's heart in searching. When they are removed
It's painful since the hands are always sharp,
Far sharper than expected; while the pearls,
On which the lover travels like a world,
Contain indelible reflections: ships
On milky seas, the future prominent
And round as the jewels themselves, and like his ghost
What every lover hates to give the most,
The chambered imprint of his heart's assent.

III.   Oxford

I read: the Sunday morning bells bemoan
Your absence. Cobblestones, the poet's gems,
Half-pearl, half-lead, make crowded rivers from
The ordinary, otherwise alone
And narrow street. I read, each sonnet steps
Whose landing I may loiter in; my fists,
Like cobblestones inside my pockets, fit
The space unfilled inside me. When I weep
Before ascending, your apartment's door—
Its diamond-peephole, its familiar frame—
Is what I fear this latticed building, lame
From its improvements, lacks. Floor by floor
I rise, as if to touch the moon, the pearl
That decorates the leaden night. I rise,
But never knock. I'm fearful that the eyes
Behind these unfamiliar doors aren't yours.

IV.   When Rafael Met Jorge

The conversation floundered for awhile.
I punched his arm. It hurt him. Locker rooms
Kept telling us that everything was cool.
The college felt uplifting, miles and miles
Of pines unable to prevent the sky,
Unable to clamp down on us. My folks
Included him in private family jokes.
His father dryly warned me not to write
The summer after freshman year. He knew.
He knew that we were friends, that friends could seem
Like lies, all honesty. The lockers gleamed
A different gleam when we returned. We knew
Two different men were walking someplace near—
Their footsteps fell upon our souls—
They drew each other near, and kissed. We saw
The open campus, our eyes everywhere.

V.   The Wedding Gifts

We didn't want a pressure cooker. Bowls
Concentrically arranged were never gifts
In which our personalities could fit.
To register our names at Bloomingdale's—
The constant kyrie of polished brass,
The melody of silver services,
The wedding china shimmering like eyes
Welled up with tears, the crystal glass
We'd never break in heated argument—
Seemed infinitely distant from the place
On our honeymoon no parent ever paid
To fly us to, where we first fucked, then went
Discovering dilapidated shacks
Where island merchants sold us precious shells
For next to nothing. Oceans gave us jewels.
The ocean, making satin from our tracks.

VI.   Our Country of Origin

I'm dreaming geographically these days.
Last night I dreamt I found our island home.
My finger traced a slick, gigantic globe
Atilt in its mahogany while days
Flashed by because I spun the world so fast.
The continents began to look obscene.
They seemed to drift apart. They seemed like stains,
Gigantically polluting stains, adrift
Upon the solitary ocean. Time,
Forever running out in my father's den
When I was just about to understand,
Had suddenly run out. The mastermind
Of every scheme was in that globe; he grinned
At me in latitudes and parallels.
Discovery, forbidden islands, hell—
To reach between your thighs was not a sin.

VII.   He Interprets the Dream

The globe that you're exploring represents
My body. I'm the island—look at me,
How much I'm like your island, my bent knees
Pathetic mountains, my cock a monument
To some pathetic dictator, my thighs
Abandoned plazas where your father's said
You'll never play. The ocean is the bed
Hart Crane is sleeping in, an ocean high
And unitary which could drown the earth.
Instead, the earth begins to swell. It's clear
You want the earth to fuck you everywhere,
The way I do, to raise you from yourself,
Transport you there—I'm here, you mustn't be
Afraid. I'm resting like an island, home
Upon this sea of sheets—your metronome
A compass in my voice, the voice you seek.

VIII.   We're Moving to San Francisco

It isn't anything that anyone
Has said. It wasn't that my parents said
They'd worry if we moved. We weren't misled
By advertisements promising the sun,
Nor thought the earthquakes sometime soon might end.
When we were drinking home-brewed beer as sweet
As we could make it, speaking honestly,
And planning preposterous futures—that was when
I saw where San Francisco somehow shone
Like fragile, prehistoric dragonflies
Entrapped like dreams in resin's amber glass
As deep as beer in amber bottles. Homes
Exist, I thought as sip by sip you drew
Me nearer in your arms, however far
A city's lights may burn, between two hearts.
I touched your glass, and found it jewelled with dew.

IX.   Translation

The words are these: queer, homo, *maricón*
In certain neighborhoods; in others, fag
Or faggot, fairy—queen when wearing drag—
Not to mention pansy, pussy, baton-
Twirler, and girl-in-your-dreams. Creative names,
But none describe us as we really are.
Take me, for instance. Married, in my heart;
A father, to my sister half my age
(But by imagination only). One
Forever unimaginable man,
A Catholic son to parents who are sad,
Or not, to see what cannot be undone:
Those pines we planted in their yard. They grow
Because they grow. My sister waters them.
The water seems like crying, now and then.
The water is our lives. It overflows.

X.   We Wear Each Other's Levi's

The cardigans you wear I wear as well.
The jeans I wear—my ghost apparent where
The faded spots will glow whenever there's
A proper slant of moonlight—when they're filled
By you, I joke I've captured you. My plot
Is simple: once I've got you wearing them
I warn you that they're my accoutrements—
To rectify the wrong, I say with feigned regret,
"I must request that you disrobe." You say,
"The cardigans I wear you wear as well,"
Dismayed. Not swayed by playing fair, I yell,
"Those clothes are mine!" "Your clothes are mine," your gay
Response. I'm unpersuaded. Buttons fly
In all directions. Undressing you at last,
The game becoming serious, how fast
I find beneath my clothes myself, your sighs.

XI. A Medical Student Learns Love and Death

The scalpel finds the heart. The heart is still.
The way it rests, suspended in his chest,
It seems a fruit unharvested, its flesh
Inedible but oddly tempting—swelled
A size I never will forget. My sleeves
Rolled up, I touch, I trace an artery—
A torturous, blockaded road—and free
The muscle from connective tissue sheaths
An unforgotten lover left in place.
My working hands become the fluttering
He must have felt; the lost anatomy
Of his emotions, gardens left in haste.
Past human bodies, no one has evolved.
With these deflated lungs, he's penitent,
He wants to say how love will never end.
I cut, and make from him the grave I rob.

XII. Denial

I want to grow you an eternal tree,
And let you live beneath it. Then, I'll sing
Autumnal melodies, a humming song
That cures without exception maladies
Of even the most lethal sort. You'll look,
And see eternally across the park,
Because in even the most common park
The sun is making grand gestures. Look,
A mirror in the sky reflects these lines
So brightly I must gaze at it. Your face
Is shining there eternally; your face
Is an eternity. You'll never die. You seem
A little tired, but—it's just a cold,
A passing cold. I know. I am your nurse,
I am singing you again this living verse,
And growing you a tree, a branch to hold.

XIII.   Towards Curing AIDS

I slap on latex gloves before I put
My hands inside the wound. A hypocrite
Across the room complains that it's her right
To walk away—to walk away's her right
As a physician. Lapidary, fine,
My patient's eyes are overhearing her.
He doesn't wince. His corner bed inters
Him even now, as she does: he hasn't died,
But he will. The right to treatment medicine
Denied is all the hollows here: along
His arms, the hungry grooves between the bones
Of ribs. As if her surgeon's thread through skin—
The rite of obligation overdue—
Could save him now. I close the wound. The drain
Is repositioned. Needles in his veins,
I leave him pleading. There's too much to do.

XIV.   Poem in Jorge's Voice

We've always known together was the place,
The only place, from which we'd walk the earth
Alive. We have no other homelands. Dirt
Was smudged across my disbelieving face—
The mud of Argentina—when I told.
The man who was my father disappeared.
Like homosexuals did there, for years
Just vanishing from parents' homes.
It is a Latin custom to disown
The only things you love, the people who
Remind you of the places you can't go,
The children whom you never really owned.
We are each other's father now. We roam
The earth in each embrace; we find the men
Who live incarcerated where the end
Of love has led them. He can keep his home.

XV. Political Poem

To write political poems, you need events
That symbolize destructive forces, love
Of something very strong, bright sedatives
You pilfer from a parent's stash, and tense,
Tobacco-smoking rivals. You must curse
To make them swear. You must advocate
Where they prohibit. You must bear the weight
Of heavy combat boots upon your verse.
(You must make light of persecution.) When
Your lover dies, a victim of their hate,
You must extend your hand, negotiate
With those who say they understand, pretend
To be like them. You must believe. You must
Forget. You must. To write political poems,
You must, you *can* create a world which seems
Both unattainable and not unjust.

XVI.   Sonnet for Our Son

Pretending fatherhood was simply sperm,
Biological concatenation,
And men and children holding hands, we hastened
To the task. Perhaps we wanted to ensure
That someone loved us at the end. Perhaps
We wanted children simply to defend
Whichever complicated arguments
They'd make to shock the world. Perhaps,
My son, we wanted naming privileges
Just once—to name you Jorge, Rafael,
The way we never really named ourselves.
We aren't ashamed. I can't explain the edge
Of people's understanding, why it stops
Where we begin. I can't explain the cliff
My dad once was, the razor Grandpa left.
Forgive us, but we love you very much.

SONG FOR OUR SON

I.   The Cycle Begins Anew

To reproduce the pattern is a noose
Whose knot I fatten with the hands I got
From ancestors who reproduced. They thought
That truth was reproduction, that a tooth
Was like a gem they'd pass along, from mouth
To salivating mouth, so hungrily
Accumulating information seed
Like spit was spilling everywhere. I mount
My lover like the gallows, solemnly.
My sweat is from their spit, I spill my seed,
I want to reproduce. My love exceeds
All hearts. The rope the generations weave
Is breaking yet is holding fast. I plunge,
My breath constricting like the noose my throat
Genetically has long disguised; then I float,
Near death. I have the vision of our son.

Rafael Campo

II. Adoption

It means, especially for us, the state
Decides if we deserve what we're denied.
We fill out forms in triplicate, apply
As well to private agencies, then wait.
Our pregnancy (it takes nine months) results
In questions of our competence. More forms
Where "wife" must be crossed out are born—
Our mailbox, more fertile than the both of us.
A social worker comes, inspects the yard.
She opens closet doors, then sees the room—
The empty crib expectant as a womb—
She looks both tired and displeased. Absurd,
Courteous questions follow: why we thought
We could be parents, what our parents said,
And whether it was fair, subjecting kids
Who'd been abandoned to, through us, such hate.

III.   He Becomes a World-Renowned Scientist and Poet

He's married to the woman of his dreams
By now. (They met, his students like applause
In classroom after classroom, near the close
Of his first semester teaching college.) Frames
Containing his diplomas, documents
Confirming his professorship, and one
Small, grainy photograph of us are strung
Across his walls. Accomplishments
I tell my friends about—the recent poems
He published (in *The Nation*), or the prize
He garnered for his work to publicize
Psychologies of oil exploration
(How penetration of the earth excites
Most men far more than passively to cull
The energy from sunlight)—almost kills
The man I was, so hungry is this pride.

IV. What Loving Parents Are

Our son will know what loving parents are.
He'll know because he'll see our fear: that some
Outrageous ignorance could tear him from
Our arms. Our son will go to seminars
And say how hard it was; our son will say
He hated us for being gay. (He'll never know
How much we wanted him never to know
Some people hate us for our love.) We'll say
"We love you, son," and other things we know
Will be impossible to understand.
Our son will see us simply holding hands.
Our son will play football. Our son will grow
And open like a flower from a fist.
We hope at day care he'll be brave and say
"I have two dads. What's wrong with love?," his face
The joy to be his loving parents is.

V. Kindergarten

They stare, but we expected stares. The shock
Comes more from how the silence resonates
Like rocks against a school bus window pane.
Expecting only stares, we overlooked
The possibility of strain like claws
Distorting every parent's smile. I want
To grab your hand, to be a supplicant
Receiving mercy from your touch. I know
We're innocent, as innocent as light
Upon its knees in playground games to brush
Their skin with golds. We have our love—not much
To recommend us. We have the vaguest fight
With fear, that fight of staring into trees
Alight with sun, that fight of finding flaws
Where beauty is. Their smiles, full of claws.
Our son is filthy. Hissing in the leaves.

VI.   My Brother's Opinion

It's not that homosexuality
Per se is wrong—you know I love you guys.
You're normal. When it comes to whether gays
In general ought to have the right to be,
Like, *parents*—now to me that isn't right.
I mean, just think about the kid. The guy
Will be a reject. All his friends will say
It's weird. I know you want to educate
The world. Okay, I understand your point.
But shit, the bottom line is that you guys
Are different. No matter how hard you try—
Believe me, I can sympathize—you can't
Be us. And God forbid the kid turns out
Like you—you said yourself you hated it!
You wouldn't want to do that to a kid.
I love you guys. I'd hate to see you hurt.

VII. I Explain Again

The orphanage imagines that a world
Exists where parents in abundance wait.
Its children were neglected, demonstrate
Behavior problems, someday shall be cured.
Its children came addicted to the drugs
Their mothers took. Its children come afraid
Of being beaten by the men who dared
To claim their right to fatherhood. With luck,
It hopes, no more shall come. And yet they did—
Some parents sold unwanted ones as slaves,
Some centuries ago. The ones with AIDS
Today die institutionalized, beds
Like knots tied loosely with grey sheets. The ones
Who shall appear in garbage cans, who might
Become tomorrow's hated parasites,
They'll know the truth: no love's the only sin.

VIII. His College Education

One day, I started saving money. Ten
Long years ago. My father once had said
The most important legacy he had
To leave his sons, besides his love, was sense.
I was impressed. An education graced
His lips; intelligence adorned his words.
I saw his university with yards
Umbrellaed under sycamores, a place
I'd send my son to learn, less place than the fate
Traditions long ago determined would
Be his. My explanation: platitudes
Expressing love, or cars to expedite
A son's departure, or strict rules which state
Exactly how a proper son behaves,
All fall far short of what he'll need. I saved
To give my son one seed to cultivate.

IX.   Birthday Party

My brother smokes a joint inside. My son
Is nine years old. My father asks to see
His grades from school. He speaks words perfectly.
My mother serves potato salad on
The paper plates that never seem enough
To bear the weight. She hands me mine, then his.
My son is with his sharp-voiced, freckled friends.
His nicest friends are partly his because
Their parents are all friends of mine. We stand
Divided by the yard. I see conspiracies,
Adults—in corners, children—and I see
My parents watching me. I have no hands,
But paper plates instead. My brother drinks
Another beer, like it was wine. I cannot pause
Again. I stride across the needle lawn—
My son looks down—then opens in a grin.

X. Gay Parents Are Neither

An unexpected sacrifice is friends
Forgetting we are gay; "society"
Is pitchforks come for the monstrosity,
Bright torches at the gate. Our last defense,
Our privacy, has disappeared with our
Community. A son means coming out
To disbelieving courts; we felt left out
When Dave and Steve, our closest friends for years,
Did not invite us to their barbecue.
A son means kindergarten father-son
Spaghetti dinners where the three of us
Will sit alone; we're left alone with few
Phone messages to light, on coming home,
Our answering machine in green and red.
A son means isolation. When we're mad,
We talk it out. Our son is all we know.

XI. · I Take Our Son to Cuba

Until I take our son to Cuba, glass
Will seem too powerful a spell to break.
The photographs will almost seem to wake
From all their years of sleep; my past,
Wherever it's reflected, will be near
But out of reach. And so it is for all
We'll never know. Our son we know we've killed
By being gay, although we've held him dear;
My island I inherited from men
Who gave me all I need but confidence
In who I am. And so it is, the dance
We do for those we love, for them, for them
We'll never know. I want to know the tree
That's poisonous, the one that's evidence
That I existed once, the one where sons
Discover who their fathers are, and speak.

Rafael Campo

XII. Gay Freedom Parade

The activists all bring along their kids,
We notice as Queer Nation marches by.
The music pulsates like the sun; the sky
Accepts this miracle of love, unleashed
Balloons diminishing until they're specks.
It's here spectacular unrest collides
With clearheaded demands for equal rights.
We follow through the crowd the massive pecs
A shirtless blonde-haired surfer type displays.
We sign petitions protesting the lack
Of funding to fight AIDS. Junked Cadillac
Convertibles glide past, their queens a way
Of saying difference is luxurious,
Delicious—abject, great. What else to say,
But that the innocence in all things gay
Belongs to every people. Even us.

XIII.   The Pediatrician Who Cured Himself

The Spanish-speaking kids he dreamed he'd cure
Of almonds in their eyes, of untold lies
The color of their skin, of scabies, lice,
And lack of vitamins—they'd never bear
The weight of sadnesses his eyes foretold,
The pain of sadnesses he'd known since when
The earth was only almonds on a tree, a bend
In some forgotten river overgrown
With reeds as tall as men. A memory
He's having lately tells him of a child
Who thinks sour nuts are medicines and trials
Before he grows—his worst fears come to be—
An almond tree inside his chest. The nuts
Come down, bore holes in him. Inside each one
A message in the language of his bones
Has grown. My son, it says you are my fate.

XIV.   The Sonnet After This Must Wait

This fantasy is ending here: a ledge
One page away from where my heart begins.
I'm home alone tonight. The distant din
Of city life is making promises
To me I doubt a city ever keeps.
One promise is to find a son for me.
Another is to keep us safe from pleas
I make myself for yesterday, for help,
Although I know I'm just remembering.
Remembering the things I never had
In case they never come. These sonnets hold
The world for me, the world I want to sing
Like lullabies to him. Someday a son
Will issue forth from me, and fill the void
I'm leaving in this world. And with this boy—
The future hurts—another promise comes.

XV.   Afterthought

Not now, Elise. I'm busy writing verse.
You know I'm terrible at math. You know
We love you just the same. It's not as though
Your brother being primogenitor
Has anything to do with how we treat
You kids. We love you equally. At worst,
We love you as a father loves his girl:
Unsure of why we're empty, incomplete
Compared to you, afraid of how we're blind
From staring at the night while you can see
Inside yourself and cry. My daughter, be
To me as Milton's daughter was to him.
Invent new math. Re-write the universe
And name the world I stumble through, a man
Who'd hurt himself if you weren't here, your hands
Upon my face. Now go. I'm writing verse.

XVI.   The Daughter of My Imagination

My country, if I were a potentate,
Would be an island and a continent.
It would be free despite its citizens.
Its mountains would resemble seas; escape
Would be impossible, because the seas
Would be as vast as mountains. Most of all,
My country would belong to me. My laws
Concerning homosexuality
And immigration would be kind and just:
Offenders would be subject to a fine
Not more in value than a poet's line,
Nor less than what my country's freedom cost.
My country, in the end, unfortunate
In being not an island nor a continent,
In being gay and full of immigrants,
Is vanishing where seas and mountains meet.

III.
THE OTHER MAN WAS ME

The End of Shame

The faggot entertained
A certain king—day in,
Day out—for many years.
Something of his pain

Was in his jester's smile.
Also present in the court:
A white magician, two small dogs,
And a noble woman once defiled

By a handsome prince, the brother
Of the faggot. The king evinced
In all of them a certain feeling.
He had never recovered

From the death of his wife,
The Queen of All-Hearts. She died
In childbirth—for the faggot,
She had given up her life

And this the king recalled each night,
Alone in bed. The faggot tried
To please him; he would kiss
The fallen noblewoman, he'd bite

And chase the little dogs,
He'd stand upon his head and cry.
The king would look displeased,
Then call for his brother in the bogs:

"My only cherished son, return!
You are forgiven of your sins.
My court is empty, since you've gone."
At this, the faggot's ears would burn

With shame. The castle, in the rain,
Looked like it was bleeding.
The noble fallen woman petted the dogs
That the magician had trained

To comfort those in need. His magic
Almost drained away, he saw
The world as it was only on days
He made love with the faggot.

He'd see a world as it is now:
An absent prince, a bloodied queen,
The love that is necessary to dream,
The faggot slowly learning how.

A Dying Art
for Eve

The physical's your art: I see
The bones inside us all beneath
Your skin. You write so burningly

It's like Italian on my heart—
A love for body raised to art,
For poetry in voice, a spark

Of knowledge free from shame. Today,
I felt ashamed; my bones became
External, ugly, bent in ways

Italian can't express. I knew
My body wasn't art. I knew
It hurt. I craved to be untrue,

An angel of destruction, bent
On finding in the firmament
Each lame-winged bird, each dying friend,

Each ugliness, if ugliness
Exists. You should belong to us,
But we're afraid. I'm not depressed—

I watch us in the magazines,
The body we're imagining,
How strangely well the models seem—

Compared to them, I'm overweight.
I'd die to eat Italian food;
I want to have my cat de-clawed

But then he'd be defenseless. Art,
You'd tell me, ready to depart
Upon your body's shrieking points

For the stars, your baldness breathtaking,
Your wings Italian poetry,
Is only this: the sudden sting,

Our hearts, our bodies razed, the fort
Abandoned, bones and paintings charred.
You live—so write! Until we're cured.

For J. W.

I know exactly what I want to say,
Except we're men. Except it's poetry,
And poetry is too precise. You know
That when we met on Robert's porch, I knew.
My paper plate seemed suddenly too small;

I stepped on a potato chip. I watched
The ordinary spectacle of birds
Become magnificent until the sky,
Which was an ordinary sky, was blue
And comforting across my face. At least

I thought I knew. I thought I'd seen your face
In poetry, in shapeless clouds, in ice—
Like staring deeply into frozen lakes.
I thought I'd heard your voice inside my chest,
And it was comforting, magnificent,

Like poetry but more precise. I knew,
Or thought I knew, exactly how I felt.
About the insects fizzing in the lawn.
About the stupid, ordinary birds,
About the poetry of Robert Frost,

Fragility and paper plates. I look at you.
Because we're men, and frozen hard as ice—
So hard from muscles spreading out our chests—
I want to comfort you, and say it all.
Except my poetry is imprecise.

Aunt Toni's Heart

A motorcycle roaring in the distance—
I sigh myself. I loved her. More than Christmas,
Even more than summer. The day before
Another family reunion, chairs
Unfolded on the lawn, like stiff fawns. Thighs
Appeared, veined watermelons—each goodbye
An afternoon of sticky kisses, sweets—

Parked cars made silver rivers from the streets.
I'd hide beneath the table where the men
Played poker in the smoky shade. They bent
Their cards. Red wine, cigars and pepperoni.
It wasn't really whispers when Aunt Toni
Sat right down beside my Uncle Joe—surprise
Is more like it—and stared into his eyes:

She smiled at him, waiting to be dealt
A hand. I remember how the green felt
Seemed perfect, clipped back, like a perfect shrine.
My family grew way outside the lines.
My grandmother would say how hard it was
For them when they arrived, each city bus
Gigantic as America, New York

Entire countries warring over work.
They hated Catholics back then, they did.
Italians too. She slowly shook her head.
"That's why you need your family," she'd say.
"Who else is gonna love you?" Which is why
I understood about Aunt Toni's heart.
My grandmother explained that it was hurt—

No, not hurt exactly, just *different*—
And that inside it was an angel sent
When she was small. The angel's name was Love,
And she was lost. "Aunt Toni's old enough
To try to find her angel now—that's all
You need to know. The rest is miracle."
I trailed Aunt Toni all day long; she fed

Me chocolate kisses from her hand. I begged
Her, catching fireflies that night, to show
Her angel-heart to me, but she said no.
My parents still won't talk about the year
Aunt Toni brought Charlene with her, blonde hair
Drawn back beneath their helmets, the wind and sun
Greedy for more gold. By then, I'd begun

To see the beauty in the world. I knew
She'd found her angel. My own heart felt new.

Aida

I've never met the guy next door. I know
He's in there—mud-caked shoes outside to dry,
The early evening opera, the glow
(Of candlelight?) his window trades for night—

I think he's ill, since once the pharmacy
Delivered his prescriptions to my door:
Acyclovir, Dilantin, AZT.
He doesn't go out running anymore.

I've heard that he's a stockbroker who cheats
A little on his taxes. Not in love,
They say—he seems to live alone. I eat
My dinner hovering above my stove,

And wondering. Why haven't we at least
Exchanged a terse hello, or shaken hands?
What reasons for the candlelight? His feet,
I'm guessing by his shoes, are small; I can't

Imagine more. I'd like to meet him, once—
Outside, without apartments, questions, shoes.
I'd say that I'm in love with loneliness.
I'd sing like candlelight, I'd sing the blues

Until we'd finished all the strawberries.
We've never met, and yet I'm sure his eyes
Are generous, alive, like poetry
But melting, brimming with the tears he cries

For all of us: Aida, me, himself,
All lovers who may never meet. My wall—
As infinite and kind-faced as the wealth
Of sharing candlelight—it falls, it falls.

The Test

Singing to himself, waiting for the voice
To call him next, he thought it out again.
He was just an accident. As a boy,
He knew there would be awful things, the men
In hot showers suspecting it was true,
His brothers never loving him again,
A balding man, alone, having Campbell's soup
For dinner. But it wasn't until after when
He'd had the surgery, and then in college
The only love he cared about, that he heard
About the virus. He'd had blood, an acknowledged
Several units—but only that one real love—sure,
There'd been some girlfriends too, two or three . . .
He laughed to himself. And doctors were surprised to see
The virus, deadly, in the tears. Where else would it be?

Allegory

Outside somewhere, beneath an atmosphere
So pure and new each breath is musical
And silent, mouth-watering, without taste,
So full of butterflies one can't imagine
Because it hurts to be so free, out there

There was a hospital where AIDS was cured
With Chinese cucumbers and royal jelly,
With herbal medicines, vaccines, colostrum.
I went there in a submarine, through space
It seemed, and I was armed with nuclear

ICBMs. I read *The New York Times*,
That's how relaxed and skeptical I was;
I sat upon the floor, my back against
The gleaming missiles. Strangely, no one else
But me was on the submarine, except

The President, whom I'd confined beneath
The lowest deck, inside somewhere where air
Was scarce and hardly breathable. One can't
Imagine what it's like to see a world
Like theirs from such a distance for the first

Time: God, was it beautiful, butterflies
And silent musical wind, the hospital
Where no one paid. I tried to give them small
Pox, missiles, blankets; they looked at me
Like I was crazy, and they asked me why

The President had been incarcerated.
There's no explaining of morality
To savages, I thought. And though it hurt
To leave, to conquer them and take with me
The royal jelly and colostrum, when I aimed

My missiles at their hospital I felt
Much better. Munching on a cucumber,
The light of the explosion brightening
My face, I couldn't help the tears, I was
So sad and happy, all at once, again.

Rafael Campo

AGE 5 BORN WITH AIDS

In Jaime's picture of the world, a heart
As big South America shines out,
The center of the only ocean. Three
Stick figures (one is labelled "me") are drawn
Beside the world as if such suffering
Could make us more objective. Jaime's bald
And has no mouth; his parents aren't like him,
They're all red lips and crazy yellow hair
And grins. There is no title for his work
Of art, except the names we give ourselves.

Technology and Medicine

The transformation is complete. My eyes
Are microscopes and cathode X-ray tubes
In one, so I can see bacteria,
Your underwear, and even through to bones.
My hands are hypodermic needles, touch
Turned into blood: I need to know your salts
And chemistries, a kind of intimacy
That won't bear pondering. It's more than love,
More weird than ESP—my mouth, for instance,
So small and sharp, a dry computer chip
That never gets to kiss or taste or tell
A brief truth like "You're beautiful," or worse,
"You're crying just like me; you are alive."

The Distant Moon

I.

Admitted to the hospital again.
The second bout of pneumocystis back
In January almost killed him; then,
He'd sworn to us he'd die at home. He baked
Us cookies, which the student wouldn't eat,
Before he left—the kitchen on 5A
Is small, but serviceable and neat.
He told me stories: Richard Gere was gay
And sleeping with a friend of his, and AIDS
Was an elaborate conspiracy
Effected by the government. He stayed
Four months. He lost his sight to CMV.

II.

One day, I drew his blood, and while I did
He laughed, and said I was his girlfriend now,
His blood-brother. "Vampire-slut," he cried,
"You'll make me live forever!" Wrinkled brows
Were all I managed in reply. I know
I'm drowning in his blood, his purple blood.
I filled my seven tubes; the warmth was slow
To leave them, pressed inside my palm. I'm sad
Because he doesn't see my face. Because
I can't identify with him. I hate
The fact that he's my age, and that across
My skin he's there, my blood-brother, my mate.

III.

He said I was too nice, and after all
If Jodie Foster was a lesbian,
Then doctors could be queer. Residual
Guilts tingled down my spine. "OK, I'm done,"
I said as I withdrew the needle from
His back, and pressed. The CSF was clear;
I never answered him. That spot was framed
In sterile, paper drapes. He was so near
Death, telling him seemed pointless. Then, he died.
Unrecognizable to anyone
But me, he left my needles deep inside
His joking heart. An autopsy was done.

IV.

I'd read to him at night. His horoscope,
The New York Times, The Advocate;
Some lines by Richard Howard gave us hope.
A quiet hospital is infinite,
The polished, ice-white floors, the darkened halls
That lead to almost anywhere, to death
Or ghostly, lighted Coke machines. I call
To him one night, at home, asleep. His breath,
I dreamed, had filled my lungs—his lips, my lips
Had touched. I felt as though I'd touched a shrine.
Not disrespectfully, but in some lapse
Of concentration. In a mirror shines

The distant moon.

Finally

Two lovers met. It wasn't lovers' lane,
But a lesser travelled road. No others came.
One lover held the other's hand. The other
Man was me. I watched as if I hovered
Far above the scene. And as the sky
Began to prickle with the stars, I tried
To understand why the other couldn't free
His heart the way the birds imperceptibly
Flew, searching for their nests. The first one said
Some words. I couldn't hear, because I bled
So loud internally—a roaring
That might never drain me, a liquid pouring
Itself out. One lover stooped, unlaced his shoes,
And dropped his lover's hand. His clothes were strewn
All throughout the reeds. They glowed like ghosts
Of lovers who had died before. Upon their throats,
The moonlight's touch was particularly white.

One lover held the other's cock. Slow, tight,
His palm confused with me sensation,
Because a lover was the one location
I had never been to. But this man knew.
And as the other's destination grew
Clearer and clearer, like finding the moon
From behind a once-obscuring cloud, the tune
Of its light all at once familiar—
So this is where the lovers came the years
I read about in school. This is always where
They came, from London-town, or county fairs.
I then imagined all the things that the earth
Hadn't held: organ music, in the hearth
Leaping flames, soul-mating, satellites—
Two lovers met. The other man was me that night.

Sonnet No. 904

This is too easy, all this afternoon
And you sitting next to me, always driving.
Did I tell you what I dreamt last night? Soon.
No, now. You know how I'm always writing—
Well, I'm sitting writing you this birthday card,
Or something meaningful. The ink is blue, thick,
And some sticks to the ballpoint. We're in the car
And you know that I love you, and huge thick
Trees sweep by, set to some wrong music
Pouring from the radio, all oldies.
Farms go, too, merely silos, a few bricks.
Farms, and more clotheslines and folding
Lawn chairs than you see in town—then, shit, we're lost.
We grope—that card was directions! Those rhymes were our past.